RIVER POEMS

An Anthology of Poetry on the Allure of Rivers

Published by

Lilly Press

All rights reserved. No part of this book may be reproduced in whole or any part or in any form or by any means without the express written permission by Lilly Press or the individual writers published within this anthology.

Cover Art, Editing, and Production by:
Judith A. Lawrence, Publisher/Lilly Press

Published by:
Lilly Press
1848 Finch Dr
Bensalem, PA 19020
Email: judithlawrence@comcast.net
URL: www.riverpoetsjournal.com

Lilly Press

Published in the United States of America

First Printing - February, 2010

ISBN 978-0-9801775-7-2

Ralph Waldo Emerson

Two Rivers

Thy summer voice, Musketaquit,
Repeats the music of the rain;
But sweeter rivers pulsing flit
Through thee, as thou through the Concord Plain.
Thou in thy narrow banks art pent:
The stream I love unbounded goes
Through flood and sea and firmament;
Through light, through life, it forward flows.

I see the inundation sweet,
I hear the spending of the steam
Through years, through men, through Nature fleet,
Through love and thought, through power and dream.

Musketaquit, a goblin strong,
Of shard and flint makes jewels gay;
They lose their grief who hear his song,
And where he winds is the day of day.

So forth and brighter fares my stream,--
Who drink it shall not thirst again;
No darkness taints its equal gleam,
And ages drop in it like rain.

CONTENTS

Anna G. Raman	A confluence of characters	8
Alexandria M. Red	Clarence	10
Christopher Tiefel	River (v)	12
Adam Berlin	Tracking Cunard	14
Bob Bradshaw	The Fighting Temeraire	15
B J Ward	For Those Who Grew Up	16
Ann Taylor	Up River	18
Glenda Barrett	The Fork of the River	19
Barbara Crooker	The Susquehanna:	20
J. Joseph Kane	thicker than	21
Bill Wunder	Holding a River Stone...	22
Bill Wunder	Reflections on the Delaware	23
C. R. Resetarits	Big River	24
Carole H. Johnston	August on Brandywine	26
Carolyn Constable	Petition To A River	27
Christopher Woods	Ceremony	28
Cynthia Hawkins	Susquehanna	29
Jake Carpenter	Generations	30
Jeanine Stevens	River Run	32
Jeanine Stevens	Shawnee Point	33
Jennifer Ackerman	Fall Flood	34
Joanne Faries	Meander	35
Jenny Root	The Language of Rivers	36
Jenny Root	Another Encore Day	38
Elijah Pringle	Rivers accept the waters	39
Dan Reynolds	Mississippi River	40
Dorla Moorehouse	Northern Phoenix	42
Ellaraine Lockie	Missouri River Roots	44
Harry Westermeier	A Reenactment ...	46
John S. Williams	Two Hometowns...	48
Karla Linn Merrifield	Approaching 0 Flow CFS	50
Ksenia Rychtycka	Cornish Cliffs and a River ...	51
L. Ward Abel	On My River	52
Mark Vogel	Breaking the surface	53
Melissa Morris	Imperfections Tickle	54
Mike Berger	The Dirty Devil	55
Neal Whitman	Big Sur Symphony	56

CONTENTS

Pamela J. Parker	Shuckswitch Road	57
Peter D. Goodwin	A Canoeist in the City	58
Regina Murray Brault	Grand Canyon, Arizona	60
Regina Murray Brault	Motive At Idaho Falls	61
Richard Roe	On the Banks of Rivers	62
Judith A. Lawrence	Point of Comfort	63
Richard Mack	River Road - Late Nov.	64
Sally Bliumis-Dunn	River	65
Robert S. King	The Underground River	66
Stephen Lefebure	Goosenecks of The San Juan	67
Tim Allen	A River Reborn	68
Thomas M. McDade	Eamon S. Quigley Recalls	69
Tom Sheehan	The Hour Falling Light …	70
Rosalie S. Petrouske	Dragons by the River	72
Vuong Quoc Vu	Song Hong: Red River	74
Wynn Everett	The Last Years	75

ACKNOWLEDGEMENTS

B. J. Ward - "For Those Who Grew Up On A River" from *Gravedigger's Birthday* (North Atlantic Books, 2002)

Pamela Johnson Parker - "Shuckswitch Road" first appeared in *qarrtsiluni*

Thomas M. McDade - "Eamon S. Quigley Recalls" previously published in *The Pawtucket Times* and *Thin Coyote*

Ksenia Rychtycka - "Cornish Cliffs and a River Near Chornobyl" - An earlier version of this poem was published in the Fall 2004 issue of *Hedge Apple*.

Barbara Crooker - "The Susquehanna" previously published in Vol No

Jeanine Stevens - "River Run" was previously published in South Dakota Review, 2008

Sally Blumis-Dunn - "River" previously published in "Talking Underwater," published by Wind Publications, 2007

Anna G. Raman

A confluence of characters

Dams can control and confine
The volume,
But not the depth of this river.
Cauvery - a profound confluence
Of characters from the past and present,
And those that will come to be,
Like that bunch of boys,
All diving and splashing,
Each wearing a single piece of loin cloth,
Or those *dhobis* a few feet away,
Who starch and shine *dhotis* and *sarees*
On the rocks and rinse,
Or that farmer scrubbing his buffalo,
Both knee-deep in the water,
Or those women who live in huts on the banks,
Who like to dip their feet in shallow water
So they shine as bright as their silver anklets,
Who then walk home carrying pots of the water,
Balanced carefully on their heads
On buns made from the ends of their *sarees*,
Or on their waists, as they would hold
little infants bubbling with energy.

Cauvery - water that flows from taps at home,
Water that lights lamps in those huts,
And here in our living rooms,
Water that they fight about over and over,
Water, that in some temple town, washes away their sins,
Water that can never be truly divided...
Cauvery - an ageless ethereal damsel
Who has purified and nurtured us for years,
Has patiently borne the mindless and the selfish,
Their sins and dirt.

Anna G. Raman

Every time I pass by train
Over that bridge, the sound of the wheels
Echoes, beckoning me
To see those kids frolicking,
The *dhobis* washing, the buffaloes bathing,
the women fetching water for cooking,
and I drop a coin down into her hands,
As I would into a *hundi* in a temple,
And pray for good luck.

dhobis - washermen
hundi - donation box placed in a temple into which people drop money as offerings to God (which is usually used for maintenance and development of the temple).

Vananski Dhobi-Wallah - Photographer - Claude Renault

Alexandria Michelle Red

Clarence

moisture
is omnipresent
in new orleans.
thunder in the
air   booms   quakes
echoes
as
vapor condenses to
hissing drops.

the mississippi
surrounds, radiates
power.

        on the river bank
clarence stands   watching
in awe.

the river flows.
        he knows
most of the city lies
below,
he remembers
when they dynamited the levees in 1927,
saving the rich part of the city,
forsaking poor blacks and whites in ninth ward
and st. bernard parrish
but he keeps
coming back
to new orleans-
she's in his blood.

Alexandria Michelle Red

he watches   waters
overflow
seeking level,
there is nothing he can do,
but be wary of the
unpredictable
       spirit of water.

1927 Flood - The Mississippi River broke its banks in 145 places, depositing 30 feet of water over 27,000 squares miles of land - Unknown Photographer

Christopher Tiefel

River (v)

i. Hudson

It was called something before
they moved over the bridge
for a new job, to start a family,
packed in plastic bags, a record.
Native American for
travels without moving.

ii. Clinton (Raritan)

Maybe we met here before. Or
after the waterfall. This is
how to feed the ducks:
save wheat crusts all week,
crumble between
fingers, throw. Like a record.

iii. Schuylkill

The river establishes the city
living between carved grooves.
Like a record. You can
add onto the edges,
commute. A new job.
I have left you sleeping with
a kiss on the forehead.

iv. Doylestown (SEPTA)

Tell the story again, like
a record: moved to work,
packed in plastic bags. Native

Christopher Tiefel

American for travel
along an alternating current.

v. Delaware

I have returned home
with a bouquet of
dandelions. From the bridge
we drop them into
muddy water. A
record, yellow flowers float
downstream.

Dandelions - Henryk T. Kaiser

Adam Berlin

Tracking Cunard

Running down Hudson River. Six a.m.
Too hot to sleep, might as well get the
cardio vascular chore done with.
Gray sky, gray water, but parallel
to Lady Liberty, her muted copper
face turned away, the orange
stack atop an ocean liner rises like
a squared sun. I've seen the ads,
heard the jingle and sure enough
as I approach, my pace made pain-
less by this grand ship that seems
a throwback, CUNARD is spelled
in bold letters under the single
orange stack that sends an aristocratic
plume, steady, not polluted looking, as
if that too were swabbed like the deck.
The passengers all awake stand
starboard side looking at New
York City's Skyline that must be beautiful
from there. My grandfather, Russian
handsome in sepia toned photographs
before people smiled for cameras,
young, Odessa educated, an Asian
looking prince, told of his crossing.
One man ladled soup. The next,
right behind, snatched the bowl.
No black tie waiters setting crystal
on white linen. It looked so slow
coming at me. I take my time
running stairs so I can follow
it back, uptown, the last two miles.
Stern letters. Queen Elizabeth Two.
Famous. From another time but not the time
I come from. No adventure when the port
is known, when the destination is home
and not a new world with promises.
This ship is faster than I thought. The current
so calm, the ride so easy, the orange stack
pulls away and I can't catch it and my breaths
come harder like his when he used his hands
to stretch furs, make a few bucks.

Bob Bradshaw

The Fighting Temeraire, Towed by a Steamer up the Thames

I'm like a horse being walked
by a stable boy, my stockings dirtied
from an exhausting race.
Soldiers retired get a pension.
I get my planks torn up,
my copper melted down.
I've become a barge of old lumber
towed by a steamer up the Thames.
Without my guns
there is no hint of Trafalgar
where I stared down booming warships.
There is no one
waiting for me at the docks.
There is only this rust-red
wash of sunset and water,
as though my rust was polluting
the Thames. I've become as harmless
as a chip of floating bark.
It's a different world from my youth.
I've been passed by, and by what,
a steamer? It sighs and heaves,
a stable boy who pulls me along
as if I were a war horse
soon to be put
down.

(*based on a painting by Joseph Mallord William Turner, 1824*)

B J Ward

For Those Who Grew Up On A River
(for Frank Niccoletti)

Brethren of muck and trout—
sultans of pike and pollywog—
clasping ropes that swung over wispy reflections
we'd shatter with our summer bodies.
We look at the world
as one long page
with fluid sentences
running across it.
I remember how the river bebopped
to its own insistent aria,
a motion whose seduction
was challenged only

by Janey's lucid summer dress
which waved to me unbearably.
I left rafts and inner tubes
for Chevies, Plymouths, anything
with a motor to take me
down asphalt estuaries,
Janey at my side,
accelerating toward an ocean
of credit and responsibility.
I felt then
the river was what I'd leave behind,
drift into the world of skyscrapers
and my children's dance lessons.
How hard it was to learn
motors fail. Romance dies.
My river compatriots,
I know you understand this:

the more rocks we hit,
the louder we sing.
Janey's long gone.
The river still kisses me.

Hippie Girl in Summer Dress - by Megan Abba

Three Rope Swing - Photographer - Caleb Reeve

Ann Taylor

Up River

I wasn't allowed where Lennie, Dad,
and his army buddy, George, shouted "Banzai!"

and winged off the cliff into the deep pool
of our Sunday White Mountain stream.

So I sank into my truck-tire tube and set off
from the flat boulder where Rose and Ma

laid out lasagna and grilled chicken.
I coursed my own rough ride through

rounded rocks' mini-whitewater,
pushed off with numbed toes, bounced

like a pinball, rubber hollow-thonking,
until the scraping beneath stopped me.

Alone, I stumbled back, tossing,
dragging the sunbaked tube.

For the picnic, I hung it from a fir limb
until I again and again deployed.

Photography by Michael Pereckas

Glenda Barrett

The Fork of the River

It was called, "Going to Water,"
when every morning, summer and winter
regardless of the weather, the Cherokee
waded into a clear, running creek or river,
and faced the east of the rising sun
before dipping themselves seven times
while reciting their prayers. For cleanliness,
they preferred to camp at the river's fork
so they could wash in one stream and use
the other one for cooking purposes.
Like the doves that light on my feeder,
I also like to ease into my morning.
My best lessons have been learned,
not in chaos, but in places of silence.
In nature I connect better with my Maker,
while feasting my eyes on Mountain Laurel,
hearing the sound of babbling brooks,
and smelling the scent of Wild Honeysuckle.
I, too, like the Cherokee seek direction
in the quietness of the morning.

Photo owned by Runningfox Moss

Barbara Crooker

The Susquehanna:

Requiem
   for Judy

It is early March, each day a little bit greener,
crocus and snowdrops already in bloom, daffodils
sending up the tips of their spears.
When summer comes, we will take you to the river,
trickle your ashes through our fingers.
You will return to us in rain and snow,
season after season, roses, daisies, asters,
chrysanthemums. Wait for us on the other side.
The maple trees let go their red-gold leaves in fall;
in spring, apple blossoms blow to the ground
in the slightest breeze, a dusting of snow.
Let our prayers lift you, small and fine as they are,
like the breath of a sleeping baby. There is never
enough time. It runs through our fingers like water
in a stream. How many springs are enough,
peepers calling in the swamps? How many firefly-spangled
summers? Your father is waiting on the river bank,
he has two fishing poles and is baiting your hook.
Cross over, fish are rising to the surface,
a great blue heron stalks in the cattails,
the morning mist is rising, and the sun is breaking
through. Go, and let our hearts be broken.
We will not forget you.

J. Joseph Kane

thicker than

saline and saltwater
are cousins.
so are canals and arteries.

in Venice,
in a gondola,
I feel like blood.

I wonder how much
oxygen I can carry.
it slips between my fingers

and against my eyes
as we drift beside sidewalks
and beneath bridges,

the old cement bones
of this city--
stiff

with the sound
of footsteps.

Venice, Italy - Photography by Keith Levitt

Bill Wunder

Holding a River Stone, Thinking of You
for C.M.

Last night, a near-full Vermont moon
rose up my windshield as it framed
a darkened ridgeline. My phone out,
I drove the mountains till my cell
had bars, and as fingers of mist
reached across the ground
in front of me, I heard you,
three hundred miles to the south,
voice cracking, grief still
holding you hostage.

This morning, the sun cuts through
a crisp autumn morning. Walking
along the muddy riverbank, I pick up
an egg-shaped stone. How beautiful
the currents have shaped you. How sad
the erosion of existence has worn you.
We resist the passage of time.
The years shed their seasons
like so many stiff leaves
falling into the cold water,
little boats carried off
on a tide of uncertainty.
How beautiful, the way
water shapes stone.
How sad, this life, and the journey
through it can become.

Bill Wunder

Reflections on the Delaware

A blood-moon squats
on the hazy horizon, looks
too swollen and heavy to rise.
Across the river, Trenton burns
with harsh urban light, its neon fire
flickers on the rippled surface;
street lamps and traffic signals distort
on the languid current. Captured
by the hypnotic shapes of light on dark
water, I'm taken back to a different river
bank watching flames consume
Ban Khe. Its gold glare shatters
into refugees of light that escape
on the river's surface. A frenzy
silhouetted against
the inferno. Impatiently,
the platoon rummages for
the inevitable stash of Charlie's
rice and AK-47s. Heated
shouts, anxious flashlight beams
probe dense bamboo and darkness
at the muddy water's edge.
A gunshot resounds
across the water. Or is it
a car backfiring in the reflected city?

C. R. Resetarits

Big River

How stay they plumb when
pasture is all hobble-hoofed
and wryly cast as steep-cut slopes
which tumble to Big River.
Cow path is hand-span wide
next trick perhaps the heads of pins.
Their bovine grace leaves fallow fields
afluttering.
The virgin glade once heifer proof
is live-wire gone since buckjump spree
so sweet, candied shoots cut uncut
shade as star-brights wink
from nebula green:
Turk's orange, violets, blues, pinks.
The herd meanders its milky ways as
shoal pebbles gurgle wet siren tones:
careful steps, sand soil shifts.
Adventure. Bounty. Oceans of threat.
One third of herd are river bound
one third demure from back pools sip
last third content in conquered glade.
Big River is careless pour and flux
cutting cliffs, fields, woods
at whim.
Brahman heifers pleasure find
wade in, wade in, udderly deep.
Big River swift winkles and panic sets.
Cows lunge benimbled knees kicking free.
Conquerors cool their ethos pays
while demure ones tuck their skills
and move en masse once back pool
quenched.
River crew dally into watercress troves
a rare rich find that they too tuck

once quenched and fed.
And so soon hoof holes fill
cress loosened swims.
Big River cuts and unattends.

Moose Bull and Cow along the River - Nave Album - 1982

Carole Herzog Johnston

August on Brandywine
   (homage to Andrew Wyeth)

Scent of wild phlox
hot and still
Brandywine creeps
between its banks

Trees lean in close
to silence
bright boats drift down
your green river

Andrew, paint me
in the scene
alone on the
rock of memory

Meadow Phlox Along the River - Photographer Ken Clark

Carolyn Constable

Petition To A River

Delaware, I drive over thee
from Center Bridge to Stockton,
Reigelsville to New Jersey,
along with crowds of tourists
from New Hope to Lambertville.

I glance up and down your corridor
witness your glory through windshield.
Instead of traversing your bridges,
I'd rather meditate along your shores,
soak up your splendor in sunshine.

On your banks of lush vegetation,
Orioles nest in Sycamores,
butterflies puddle on tow path.
Tiny Deptford Pink wildflowers
mingle with Blue-Eyed grasses.

As your current surges forward,
I sense your power.
You dance headlong toward the sea.
Constancy of your movement,
relaxes and reassures me.

I'm grateful I live near you,
to walk along your riverbed,
hear the melody of your waters,
experience serenity a river brings.
O'Delaware, may I absorb your peace.

Christopher Woods

Ceremony

Many years later, when he would have time to reflect, he would recall this narrow path, how it grew from the wider dirt road and followed the river.

And all along this path and the riverside were those extraordinary palms, guiding his every step.

His feet were blistered from many weeks of walking. Nearing the village, he had time to rest. He recalled the long walk, the suns and moons he had passed beneath. He remembered how his frazzled brain had coaxed him to continue.

He considered the river, and the palms. How, at long last, he entered the village and rested in the plaza. How, after bowing, he offered his worn feet to the shaman with the great saber, the holy man who fed pilgrims' feet to the palms at the riverside.

And he considered how things, broken and not, seemed to have a life and a faith all their own, a kind of sequence that moved from one year into the next.

Mekong River

Cynthia Hawkins

Susquehanna

I open my mouth in the rain
and consider the weight
of the Susquehanna
in the lungs.

Lights of Lourdes Hospital
push down between trees,
glow all the way
to the other bank.

Through the leafless fringe of limbs
ribbed shadows over water expand
with the swell of a river
rising in the four-day rain

that keeps us tasting
the wet lips of all who are missing.
Cupped puddles in the palms
speak of loss, of rain,
and the body in the river.

I look for the drowned boy,
everybody looks, look for his long
back to surface and split a river in two.

The Susquehanna swallowed
all sound with the body.
We all wait, rain on tongues,
for knuckles to arch up
white with a wave
and exchange proof for silence.

Jake Carpenter

Generations

She runs
to me with sunlight
in her hair
beaming from her eyes
and she runs past
and hops to the river
so I turn and watch her
crouching on the edge
poking her fingers
through the surface to feel
the wetness and the
coolness.
I look past her
from where the river comes
it stretches across
the Midwest flatness
as far as I can see
until the details fade away
the breeze blown shimmers
of blue and black and brown
at my daughter's feet
in the distance look smooth
and where the river drains the sky
as it appears
the million greens of the trees
turn white then blue
like haze
but my daughter splashes
and looks back at me
with the colors of a sunset
on her cheeks
She likes the feel
of the breeze drying
her wet arm

and she looks up the river
just ahead
where the water bends
out of sight
and where the unstoppable current
rushes to.

Little Girl Playing on the Beach - Photographer - Erica Hayward

Jeanine Stevens

River Run

We must make more of Autumn
   than covered bridges and red aspens.

I want to follow where the Truckee
   runs down to the Carson Valley Plain,

see night-white ruffles reflect ethereal birds
   skipping in warm, sweet buck brush,
      flitting ripples, carrying wings,

flowing under Reno—neon and glitter,
   and the California Zephyr's silvery tracks.

Water breaks, broken water.... leeching
   fenced farms, but still determined,
      overflowing, exposing brittle bison bones.

Emerging from purple ceanothus thickets
   wild rabbits blanket my headlights
      fiery orange—eye-shine!

Then, the river fans out quiet,
   lapping tufa formations at Pyramid Lake,

old shards polished bright—
   ghost dancers drinking deep.

Jeanine Stevens

Shawnee Point
Southwestern Ohio

Not long ago, we climbed the steep
hardwood forest in a green
and gold October. Just half way up,
where the land leveled out,
a dwelling site restored: fire pits
and ceremonial circle. I heard
quiet feet follow me
to the lookout, the high bluff
over the Ohio River.
It was early, the benches still wet.
Standing in yellow grass, I looked
to the west, Indiana and Kentucky
glistening emerald with a late harvest,
then, to the east where immigrants
came, old relatives, farms lost
in the Revolutionary War,
seeking fertile bottomland.
I stood with the Shawnee, watched
the first boats come downstream.

Boats in Locks on the Ohio River   -   Ohio Historical Society

Jennifer Ackerman

Fall Flood

I'm down here at the Winnebago River
Came down to hang out on the swinging foot bridge
and watch the river run over the rocks
But the river and rapids are gone
Been replaced by this shallow, funny lookin lake
With trees and light poles growin out of it
Looks like the geese sure do like the new lake
They're havin second thoughts about the south
But not me
That dock over there's inviting me to launch a canoe
and flow south with the water
And that old time train whistle blowin in on the south wind
Transports me to earlier days
I can just imagine
A big black coal engine chuggin into town
Winds pickin up
This oak leaf tangled in my hair brings me back to my day
So I sit down in the middle of the foot bridge
to record these observins
And I find myself staring through these metal bars
Man this is my kind'a prison
Hold me here like an autumn leaf
Hold me here till I turn a brilliant red
Then release me on the wind to fly to wherever I need to be next
Thank you, thank you my dear good mother earth. Thank you.

Joanne Faries

Meander

many river rapids
surprise waterfalls
accelerated emotion
leaves gasps of
relief at the end of the ride

one river begins
breaks into tributaries
of trouble and
tumbled heartache

all rivers erode
drag sediment and sentiment
until the ferried stick on a sandbar

an underlying river
glacier melt cool
roiling Amazon hot

burbles in the soul

Root

Language of Rivers

"When I wanted to protect my land, I learned there are no boundaries." — Johnny Sundstrom, Siuslaw Institute

I speak in a river tongue, my mouth
alive with salmon, my land alive
with conversation. Forest and river.
Fish who travel the waterways
home. Muscle and memory.

I listen to this land, dream
bass notes of current and stone.
When I dreamt in warm soprano
the salmon had stopped returning.
I was silent, stagnant. To protect
my land I had to leave.
I had to travel like salmon
beyond boundaries. I left
my watershed for the city
with its stone monuments and
state houses, its straight lines.

I had to learn a new language
but when I spoke my river
spoke through me and filled
my mouth with its journey
speaking of grit and silt,
spawn and return. Of flood plain
and snow melt and drought.
Of mudslides and log jams,
riprap and trampled banks.
Across states and continents
I spoke to people who understand
the language of swirl and tide,

delta and waterfall, but also
of human law. Slow
accommodation, bartered
cooperation. Still, together
in conservation our rivers
joined. I felt the salmon
fill my mouth again. I returned
and was no longer silent.
I lay down in the river and spoke.

Salmon River - Photography by Dave Eriqat

Jenny Root

Another Encore Day

*[Sauvie Island the near horizon,
a single jet flies low to the east
and Canada geese fly west.]*

Down the gangway and along the dock
a woman and man walk on the afternoon
wake, nervous as first graders
in a Christmas play. Past three
homes floating in the channel
and then they come to an empty slip
where his house would go come May.
The arms of the slip embrace
the waves southeast to northwest. And
she wonders, has he seen the rainbow
stretching bank to bank, gussying up
the clouds, fluttering on wave and breeze?
A ribbon curtsies with the rain and sun
for another encore day.

Rain the scene-stealer puts on her makeup,
dresses and undresses before
the sighing setting sun.

And the man, unobserved,
observes the starring queen
in his play—exquisite backdrop
fluttering behind her
of indigo, maize and thunder.

Elijah Pringle

Rivers accept the waters

Brought to them by streams
By rain whatever flows to them
They carry without complaining

Creeks bring their offerings
Down mountains thru valleys
Never slowing to rest

Rivers accept what is brought

To them, the waste,
The impurities, the noxious
Rippling all the way to the sea

To the ocean; rivers
Carry all that flows in them
They do not have the stillness

Of lakes surrounded by land
Where sediment floats to the
Bottom, rivers accept all

Offerings sacrificed into them
Gushing forth babbling out a
Warning

      if you do not move
you will be swept away
into the quickly collecting current
which gathers all that would not
retreat to the banks

                  Rivers admit
All debris just to accept the water

Dan Reynolds

Mississippi River

Under the shadow of the dam
Moving in the water
Roiling

The fish are riding a tumbling current
Motionless in the sun
All gone blue and shining
Underwater

The sheepshead,
The gar
Body like a spindle

In the center of the river
White bass running
Catch them
Learning how to use the jig
Just this length
Under the bi-colored bobber
The old man showed us how

We saw him put old blue gills' guts on the treble hook
The rock for a weight
Down deep
And the rod bent down
And he took his fish
Big catfish
Making his white stomach huge impression
In the sun

On river of all time
Mississippi
Barges moving silent
All time river

Magic of the floating barges
In all sunrise
Misting
River of my heart
Mississippi

Freshwater Catfish Photo by drrj

Dorla Moorehouse

Northern Phoenix

West of the Mississippi,
    nobody under thirty
    knows about the
    Cuyahoga River fire
    of 1969.
Somehow, flaming water
    more putrid than hell
    has fallen out
    of cultural memory.

Back home, even toddlers
    know the story, the lesson -
    they promise to do better.
They promise to clean
    up messes that
    should never have been made.

Back home, there's
    a sort of pride -
    yes, we almost killed
    a river, we almost
    burned down a city
But look -
    we resuscitated everything.

Back home, there's
    a sense of hope -
    the jobs are gone,
    the people are fleeing -
But once, it was
    even worse, once
    we had to keep
    the river from going
    up in smoke

Dorla Moorehouse

Surely if we can
    fix an ecosystem
    we can fix
    the economy, we
    can rise again.

West of the Mississippi,
    everyone my age
    thinks Cleveland is drowning
    is one breath short of dead,
Not knowing
    we're a special breed,
    a Northern Phoenix -
    born of water,
    rising from pollution.

Cayuga River Fire Aftermath

aine Lockie

Missouri River Roots

I looked like an eight-year old crucifix
flying off the garage
Arms extended with a kite on each

The dreams began in recovery
When codeine-powered flying
replaced walking on a broken leg

There I soared over the Missouri Breaks where once
a bald eagle snatched a baby blue heron so close to me
I could see the eagle's yellow eyes

I became that eagle and through her eyes I saw
the savage and sacred annals of Montana Badlands
The six Indian tribes who worshipped my ancestors' feathers

Sandstone cliffs that suffered with me the long hard winters
Lewis and Clark who drank the river water beside me
Trappers and pioneers ripping, like me, flesh from waterfowl

These eyes saw farsighted my loyalty to the world
I tasted the carrion I cleansed from it after every war
Felt the weight of Augustus' soul that I carried to heaven
The burden of a national emblem

These eyes saw nearsighted the betrayers below me
Who carried rifles, drove vehicles that collided with me
Built power lines that electrocute spread wings
Poisoned prairie dogs, wolves and coyotes that I then ate

Decades later the dreams expand to visions
Protestant beliefs to reincarnation
I choose a bald eagle as my next destination
Judasas and Delilas who walk the earth be damned

Ellaraine Lockie

Already I eat sushi, fly the world in airplanes
Swim with a seven-foot arm span
Look for those yellow eyes in lovers

Eagle in Flight

Harry Westermeier

A Reenactment - River of Symbols

Perched on a bench with eager anticipation
That is the extent of my participation
On this historic day the seventh of June
In the year two thousand and nine
When Four hundred years ago to the day
Henry Hudson sailed the good ship Half Moon
Around this bend or river wind
Or so people on the river say.

I sit on Constitution Island and across the way
Is the actual west point of the Hudson River
Behind it are the battlements of West Point,
The Academy. As I sit watch children play
I think someday they with children will sit and point
To the same spot and will tell of the river
And of the day they saw the Half Moon replica
Sail up the Hudson with all its flotilla:
The Onrust, the Clearwater, Mystic Whaler and such
The Half Moon and the Onrust fly the flag of the Dutch
While The Mystic Whaler and Clearwater fly the stars and stripes
The others fly four hundred year banners and signs of all types.

Cannons salutes from West Point heralds the coming
Of the sailing ships on a nearly windless day.
I watch as they sail by the bend at the Island.
Aloft is a man in the crow's nest. Some others along the ship
Stand and wave in their orange tee shirts of modern day.
While I sit and watch, my sixty three years of aches and pains
Fade into the back of my mind as I watch with other eyes, I rewind
History for a moment in time and space and watch our story entwine
Me and the Hudson on a day in June;
Me along the Hudson watching the Half Moon;
At any age It is great to be a part of History.
At any age It is great to enjoy life's mystery.

How we come and go like the river but
the river remains and marks the change
Yet its essence remains unmarked by chains
That was in our revolutionary war of glory
And that, my friends, is yet another river story.

Half Moon - Photography by Harry Westermeier

John Sibley Williams

Two Hometowns on the Same River

At a dear friend's wedding,
our backs to the twirling, kicking dancers
erupting in white satin smiles,
we spoke- her father and I-
of the rivers running, now unseen,
beneath our hometowns,
the young trees that speak
for the myth of underlying water,
with no other indication
but old men juggling half-remembered stories
in churches and bars.

Not ten years before his village,
nearly nameless in Romanian wood
and deep mountain shadows,
introduced in a nuptial ceremony
pavement and power lines,
and he could feel beneath him
the river drying a little,
the tree thirsting.
With so much now to discuss
conversation was lost
in the great unspeak,
the perfect unison of lip-movement.

To each river its flood.
Each flood its rising water mark
and disembodied, drifting branches.

In its own way
my city too is not a word
and cannot be unwritten,
not a body buried in a shallow,
well-marked geometry of grass.

John Sibley Williams

The river, we agree, must be deeper
and littered with other kinds of bones.

Where yesterday leads us, like a river.

Our cigarettes popped, fumed, spoke
like a river.
And one answer cracked behind us
under the groom's foot.
I overheard someone say
eternity is a failed attempt
to reassemble glass.
Acceptance, she continued, is leaving the shards alone.

Portland Oregon

Karla Linn Merrifield

Approaching 0 Flow CFS

Invincible September stalks summer,
advancing to seal shut the season with frost.

How may I grasp the abundant warm moisture
of the San Juan River where I floated last June?

How breathe wisps of nebulosity?
I close my eyes to shutter recollections

of silt swirling midstream and in eddies that
encircled me with glinting bronze waters,

as strands of my hair wildly swept in upcanyon winds—
a nimbus of silver. Now the memory is sepia-tarnished.

And what of the polished limestone oval I purloined
from shore, my smooth souvenir, the one I clasp

in my dry palm as if to recreate the current's embrace?
I hold captive these millions of calcium carbonate molecules,

but they whirl away from my hand, dispersing
the wan halo of San Juan's eons of labor.

Autumn begrudges its glimpses of ephemerality;
evaporation dissipates my confluence with the river.

The volume of a river's flow is measured in cubic feet per second (cfs).

Ksenia Rychtycka

Cornish Cliffs and a River Near Chornobyl

This river is nothing like the waves
embracing the jagged slab on Land's End
where we sat before the onslaught of the storm,
heads bowed against the sun. We walked through Cornwall
on feathers of soil and grit, stared at crumbling castles
of our own make-believe past, never mind
dragons breathing fire in lightning strikes of ochre.
Our smiles were fresh as starched dresses pulled hot
from the iron. We swayed to the whistle of a hundred
trains that took us north and south, crisscrossing
the paths etched against our flesh while we learned to breathe
in tandem, count each footstep like foreign words
soft and sweet to our ears until the screech
of the train wheels jolted us back
and we were ordinary once again.

This river is still and sparkles with the lustre of a life
well-lived, the best wine saved for the banqueting hour
at a table carved from the tallest oak in the world.
I walk alone along its bank, peer at ghost silhouettes
of Viking ships a thousand years past,
plying this water pathway from the barren north
to the gold of a city decked in splendor.
The locals speak of *kohannia*, a lilt that catches
me unaware, draws me close to a dance
that even I from a far-off land can comprehend.
Yet the river weeps in places far beyond the bends
of easy reach and camera's eye, somewhere
far below the swirl of a wave
tossing the sailboats high and fast.

L. Ward Abel

On My River

I know the river
know the name it gives only me
in my dark night.

I know its rumbles, something
much larger than I. I
hear the moving.

It gives, I receive
a continuance of shadows
lit by real world chutes.

The world tries to define everything
like the waters, like me,
but I don't need that.

Cover the windows.
There's a crescent in the front yard.
Gather for midnight

because the big river kneels
it rolls with plans of its own
and still ends up salt.

Just salt.
Seasons are spinning.
Trust

nothing, no one.
See, everybody's in their own
canoe.

Ksenia Rychtycka

Cornish Cliffs and a River Near Chornobyl

This river is nothing like the waves
embracing the jagged slab on Land's End
where we sat before the onslaught of the storm,
heads bowed against the sun. We walked through Cornwall
on feathers of soil and grit, stared at crumbling castles
of our own make-believe past, never mind
dragons breathing fire in lightning strikes of ochre.
Our smiles were fresh as starched dresses pulled hot
from the iron. We swayed to the whistle of a hundred
trains that took us north and south, crisscrossing
the paths etched against our flesh while we learned to breathe
in tandem, count each footstep like foreign words
soft and sweet to our ears until the screech
of the train wheels jolted us back
and we were ordinary once again.

This river is still and sparkles with the lustre of a life
well-lived, the best wine saved for the banqueting hour
at a table carved from the tallest oak in the world.
I walk alone along its bank, peer at ghost silhouettes
of Viking ships a thousand years past,
plying this water pathway from the barren north
to the gold of a city decked in splendor.
The locals speak of *kohannia*, a lilt that catches
me unaware, draws me close to a dance
that even I from a far-off land can comprehend.
Yet the river weeps in places far beyond the bends
of easy reach and camera's eye, somewhere
far below the swirl of a wave
tossing the sailboats high and fast.

L. Ward Abel

On My River

I know the river
know the name it gives only me
in my dark night.

I know its rumbles, something
much larger than I. I
hear the moving.

It gives, I receive
a continuance of shadows
lit by real world chutes.

The world tries to define everything
like the waters, like me,
but I don't need that.

Cover the windows.
There's a crescent in the front yard.
Gather for midnight

because the big river kneels
it rolls with plans of its own
and still ends up salt.

Just salt.
Seasons are spinning.
Trust

nothing, no one.
See, everybody's in their own
canoe.

Mark Vogel

Breaking the surface

Spring sun split by trees
spills light on silver green water.
Mica sparkles on the river floor
amidst black rocks and swirl.

The first cast, cold and sleepy,
aims for waiting fish, the fly moving fast
to shadows hiding depths, the current
carrying, pushing, catching light.

A trout grabs and runs,
an assured pushing for freedom,
mad leaping into air and sun,
twisting color alive and clean.

In quiet warming sun, the day suddenly mature,
this New River once again transparent,
I admire the stilled fish breathing quietly
in the palm, and release.

Already I check the current for potential,
stalling (still), noting the snails on the rocks,
waiting for the water to forget,
until a shiver says *now*.

The picture from a distance—
hemlock, rhododendron, frozen clouds,
a rocky river, white sun in the shallows,
the statue in the swirl—eyes locked on water.

Melissa Morris

Imperfections Tickle

From my seat on the bouncing coach bus
Looking through the smeared tempered glass
The surface of the water was crushed velvet
Cascading contently along the landscape for miles
The same as the fabric from my mother's cardigan
The one that I thought was so beautiful and elegant
The one she wore until the elbows were thin
And velvetless, not really very luxurious at all
The one I wanted to wrap around me and
Shimmer in the setting sunlight
Rippled, plush
Shadowed, serene
Enchanting
Let its imperfections tickle my fingertips

Not sure where we were or which river it was
Only that it was somewhere between Salem, Massachusetts
And home
I didn't see signs or landmarks
I was too embarrassed to ask and admit I didn't know where we were
No one else seemed to watch the river or even notice it
They were all asleep
Or reading
Or caught in a daydream

So, until the road veered to the left and
We clumsily merged with other busses and minivans
And the river began flowing away from me
Flowing back, determined towards Salem
It was my crushed velvet
A little bit of magic, wrapped all around me

Mike Berger

The Dirty Devil

We were parched;
raspy voices and bleeding lips

Red sandstone punctuates the
sage flats.
Searching respite
from sun.

In a gorge there below
a murky ribbon winds. Snaking
Its way. Is that stream
more water than dirt?

They called it a river but
with a stiff
wind, I could spit across.

With a
small entrenching tool,
we dug
a hole to make a pool.
We diverted
some ugly gray
water.

Praying it would
settle before it
would evaporate. We drank
that water.
It was sandy
and pukey warm.

We splashed each other like
giddy kids.
The Dirty Devil doesn't
look like much,
but at the least it's wet.

Neal Whitman

Big Sur Symphony

Sitting on a twig chair,
in the middle of the Big Sur River,
behind the River Inn,
I listen to the running water.

At first I hear one gurgling sound.
Then, looking at a single stone,
I can hear water
flooding over its round top.

Next I see a sharp and angled rock
and pick out its own sound,
as water splits left and right,
moving moving, around around.

Some boulders ride high, others low,
each player in tune.
I sit, look, and listen
to the symphonic river run.

Big Sur

Pamela Johnson Parker

Shuckswitch Road

The summer I turned six,
The Mississippi
Flooded our farm,
Following us to the second
Story. The third night
We got out by boat,
Oaring off in a slant
Of rain, leaving the car,
The burley crop, the chickens,
The family Bible,
And the house like a girl
Waist-high in water,
White skirts wavering
On its surface.
The neighbors on King's Hill
Had coffee and quilts, holding
Them out like hands. Inside,
There was a fire, feather
Pillows; the cat had her kittens.
Their mewling soprano
Sang me to sleep. And later,
In fever, I dreamed
The dream I still have
When it rains: a country
Of sand, drought; camels;
Children, the tender swelling
Of their bones; small streams
Struggling into current.

Peter D Goodwin

A Canoeist in the City

He has achieved distinction in the City
  but several lifetimes ago
he was a small boy living along the Amazon River
  where there are no roads
no electricity and few services
  just that magnificent river
where he paddled to school
  in a dugout canoe
listening to the sounds that surround
  sweet songs, raucous calls of the forest
the swoosh and splash of fish and dolphins
  the gurgle as the canoe glides along the dark waters
sensing the current, the mood of the river
  two hours in the morning
  two hours in the afternoon
unless the weather was really bad
  then he slept in the school
listening to rain pelt and rattle the tin roof.

Years ago
  he abandoned the canoe
        for the bus
for the plane
  for the subway
        in the City
where he could be true to his talents.

He never lost his love for the River
  nor the joy he felt paddling a canoe
a craft so gentle so graceful so practical
  that on one trip back to the River
he bought a canoe
  a well built and well seasoned craft
shipped it to New York

where it rests in his room
and never touches water.

Sometimes, when I need
       to feel at peace with the world
       I sit in it and dream.

Man in Canoe - Getty Images

Regina Murray Brault

Grand Canyon, Arizona

This is how I choose to enter my sixties --
by being the last of twelve to board a raft
and the only one wearing a life vest
when our guide pushes off
to challenge the Colorado River.
I take only calculated risks.

I know a man who left the monastery
because in the end, he believed our ancestors
had gills, and one day crawled to dry land
in a place exactly like this.
I pondered that idea for awhile, concluding
that I need more evidence before I buy it.

There are some still unanswered questions
roiling in my head as I dig into this rubber raft
that bounces through white water. But, of this I'm sure,
I don't want to know about the family likeness
in amniotic fluid and river water, nor what
lurking secrets hold their breaths beneath these rapids.

I've come this far without that information
and quietly exhale the thought of anything
that could make me lose my grip at this late date.
My plan is simple; hang on to this raft
to the end of my run. Survive.

Regina Murray Brault

Motive At Idaho Falls

The ducks of Idaho ride river rapids
their webbed feet hanging loose
as they bob and turn
in currents that sweep them
toward the falls.

From a bench near the bank, I crumble
brown crust of a sandwich
as if it is the reason
I have come here --
to lure ducks from disaster.

But they, already airborne
are headed toward the other bank
to families of picnickers
who offer more.
My feet scuffle the dirt

where others' feet have scraped
the earth beneath this bench
and killed the grass
leaving evidence that they were here
like me, for their own reasons.

Richard Roe

On the Banks of Rivers
    Banks of the Oise at Pontoise – Camille Pissaro

An old man looks across the river
at a stable, a blacksmith's shop, a two-story
white house. Beyond a stand of poplars
a long chimney sends gray smoke
into a sky that's good weather blue
with flat-bottomed white clouds.
The river looks scenic, village bucolic
with colorful boats tied to dock posts.
A woman under her umbrella walks
in the receding distance, her head turned,
looking back at the poplars and chimney smoke.
Who wouldn't want to look back, the river,
new factories, leisure time, goods sold at market?
And paintings, beautiful some said, what we want.
They won't see the refuse that clogged French
rivers, nothing that would detract from a scene
that's made to sell pictures.

In my later days, I will drive across the Ohio River
and stand down the hill from the college
where I studied Economics, Biology
and Modern History. A woman walking
the other way will turn back, and we will talk
about boathouses; docks where barges unloaded
sand, rock, and coal; hotel bars, old pottery works,
good places to eat. We will know the history
of buildings torn down, streets closed down,
and trees cut down because of disease.
Trees and parks will shield a metal alloy plant.
The sky will be blue, clouds white as laundry.
A helicopter will pass overhead, someone
taking photos of the river as a peaceful
and flowing thing for postcards I will
send to friends, no sign of fish kills,
what hides beneath the water's surface.

Judith A. Lawrence

Point of Comfort

In the bare bones of
stones, rocks, stick branches
and hollow tree trunks
I find unexpected comfort
walking along the rambling
brush-strewn paths
overlooking the wide
gray-olive-green
flowing heaviness
of the Delaware river
deplete of geese,
the absence of catfish
rippling the surface,
the lone boater departed,
nature and man
having given up its summer radiance
to this bleakest of winters,
its choppy texture chugging along
past tiny cottages dotting
craggy river banks
tucked between the crumbling walls
of factories long forgotten,
its distinctive rhythms
echoing through my bones
having grown from sapling
matured, gnarled
and weathered
with the gravity of this river.

Richard Mack

River Road - Late November

the road and the river run together into the canyon
right here where Hoffer's round barn used to stand
November is real here, and cold

black bulls and gray boulders lie together
near the leafless pale of cottonwoods
in a roadside pasture

a heron stands where the river bends
its long legs lost in the swaying reeds
and marbled swirl of the Wallowa

a silent coyote walks a side hill
padded feet breaking the frosted grass
and eyes looking back soft as night

pale horses walk in thin mist at water's edge
spectors floating in the slow smoke
of burning incense

tamaracks die the winter death
and walk like scattered
old men on the ridge tops

and then mountains soften to hills
and rock becomes furrowed ground
as the road finds Cricket Flat and then Indian Valley

a brief, slender rain caresses the road
until, finally, the pewter sky opens to sunlight
like the ending of a dream

Sally Bliumis-Dunn

River

Imagine standing
on a footbridge above
a river,
the water rushing
over the rocks,
and though the water
is clear,
it is moving
very quickly,
so you cannot
clearly see
the textures
of the rocks.
You cannot see
the shadows,
tiny as heads
of pins, or fine
as arcs of eyelash
on the surface
of the moss,
or gray lines
of fracture
on the contours
of the quartz;
not flakes
of silver mica
or the occasional
feldspar pink,
because the river
though clear
is moving very
quickly.

Robert S. King

The Underground River

On its back is a plugged farmer's well
where his girls chattered and sang,
let down their long ropes of hair,
drawing up the most vocal water.

An indoor faucet plugs, unplugs city water now.
The world comes in metered from remote.
The TV chatters; the girls are on mute.
Father falls asleep to the mantra of microwave.
The family garden grows in the nearby Wal-Mart.

Mother, had she seen the currents and circuits connecting,
would likely have pulled the plug, fallen into the well's
deep journey, not into the bone-cold ground near the house
where birds drink the dewdrops on her headstone
as if to drink her purest tears,
while ghosts of rainwater rust in nearby barrels.

The girls only date cable repairmen, mechanics,
and plumbers, those who have the tools
to tighten the leaking and the loose,
to keep everything running in place.
There are no more animals to feed, save themselves.
Every year the birds know fewer songs.

Under a remodeled house and its softer beds,
the underground river quenches the dead
but sweats the dreams of those who live in wires.
Still carrying a tune, still carving out its future,
the river beneath is always beginning, always arriving,
its headwaters, its mouth full of the same eternal song,
lyrics of a language they no longer understand,
a gurgle or a death rattle now in their plugged and distant ears.

Stephen Lefebure

Goosenecks of The San Juan

Guides may be forgiven the omission
Of this deep meander flowing where
The pavement does not pause and barely strays.
Stopping here enhances recognition

Of our own endeavors to forswear
The future with a thousand vain delays.

We cannot avoid the strong suspicion
That this river is a kind of tear

In space, a place where time can flow both ways,
Because that is exactly our condition,
Turning endlessly while we prepare
A past we will remember all our days.

San Juan River meandering upstream from the Colorado River

Tim Allen

A River Reborn

Near the falls a forge was born
source springs of iron; pouring into;
a rapid river of steel
flowing along the river
shooting out over the precipice
then falling into the red river of rust
down below
surrounded by brown fields
and rust belt towns.

Then, the greens keepers came
starting out new, cleaning the springs
of wind props.
the river becoming clean
filtered through sand; silicon blue as
the river's true color
silicon capturing the sun.

the wind and the sun
no longer subtle destroyers
of inert iron and steel.
The greens keepers
re-builders retrofitting
the land and the river
pulling out the poison
and bringing back the people
life renewed and constantly renewable

Thomas Michael McDade

Eamon S. Quigley Recalls

My father was a canal digger.
Long time ago I would point
out what he dug to my niece Cora.
When I got sickly-old overnight
her mother took me in.
All my working life
I walked the mules
that towed coal barges
along my old man's trench.
Never rose higher than that.
Never married or complained.
I had a weakness for rum
and the houses along the canal
that Cora's teachers said were inns.
When she wrote
a towpath flower theme
she chose the umbrella plant
which made my eyes tear
like coal dust had blown.
I pictured the single white flower hiding.
Cora called it a May apple
like my late friend Maddy
who'd been the star of the pink
house by the falls.
I used to rip up umbrella plants
to decorate the mules.
Cora wrote that the bloom was smack
in the crotch of the plant.
She copied that from a wildflower book.
Made me blush but I only remembered
Maddy with a white blossom
in the V of her blouse
near the spot where my father dug
his first lazy spadeful.

Tom Sheehan

The Hour Falling Light Touches Rings of Iron

(at the First Iron Works of America, Saugus, MA)

You must remember,
Pittsburgh is not like this,
would never have been found
without the rod bending right here,

sucked down by the earth.
This is not the thick push
of the three rivers' water
hard as name calling…

Allegheny, Susquehanna
and the old Monongahela,
though I keep losing the Ohio.
This is the Saugus River,

cut by Captain Kidd's keel,
bore up the ore barge heavy
the whole way from Nahant.
Mad Atlantic bends its curves

to touch our feet, oh anoints.
Slag makes a bucket bottom
feed iron rings unto water,
ferric oxides, clouds of rust.

But something here there is
pale as dim diviner's image,
a slight knob and knot of pull
at a forked and magic willow.

Tom Sheehan

You see it when smoke floats
a last breath over the river road,
the furnace bubbling upward
a bare acidic tone for flue.

With haze, tonight, the moon
crawls out of Vinegar Hill,
the slag pile throws eyes
a thousand in the shining,

charcoal and burnt lime thrust
thick as wads up a nose.
Sound here's the moon burning
iron again, pale embers

of the diviner's image loose
upon the night. Oh, reader,
you must remember,
Pittsburgh is not like this.

Saugus River Loading Pier - Saugus Iron Works Photos

Rosalie Sanara Petrouske

Dragons by the River

All afternoon along the Yellow Dog River
    dragonflies hover,
sunlight shooting off their wings.

They fly in pairs, skim low,
    then rise languorously,
      while beneath them
 greenish water ripples.

Trout jumps up, disturbed from sleep,
    flips once, disappears.
    Small brown butterflies,
sprightly wood nymphs, cluster on red berries.

Day draws into late afternoon,
    shadows leap like poplars.
Moss makes a quiet cover for the whitetail doe
    edging closer.

Sitting on a rock near the river,
    I breathe in and out carefully.
On a stone next to me, a small frog crouches,
    cocks its head to one side.

I don't move my foot, or hand, or blink an eye.
Little frog croaks low in his bulbous throat,
    then higher still he sings.

Frog's voice joins the crickets and bees buzz.
Grasshoppers snap their legs in long grass.

In my head, I write lyrics to my companion's
notes. Each word scattered like phlox petals
    amongst fiddlehead ferns.

Rosalie Sanara Petrouske

All around us, the silver dragonflies flit to the tempo.
One rises, circles, before caught
       on an updraft.

For a moment, they hang in mid-air, motionless.
Then ascend
       one after another,
              after another.

Frog sitting on river rocks - Photographer - Cathy Keifer

Vuong Quoc Vu

Song Hong: Red River

I had a dream I returned
to my mother's village
on the banks of a great river;
its water was red and thick
with silt. In this dream, I fell
into the river, the water tasting
metallic, strong with iron.
I awoke and found myself
with a heavy nosebleed.

There was no way to stop
the bleeding. I held my nose
with my fingers; I wiped blood
from my face, yet it kept
streaming and pooled
in the palm of my hand--
that color- I might as well
have been holding rose petals,
the red of ochre dust, of fire!

That blood red, how familiar, deeper
than bone, how fundamental it felt
to me. That strong iron smell,
that warmth where it pooled like mud
in my hand, my mother must know it,
and her father and mother,
and those before them have known it--
red soil, water from a river; thick with silt.
Their feet knew that red mud warmed in the sun,
the mineral smell of a plowed field.

And when the rainy season came,
the river flooded its banks
and overflowed, its red silt bleeding
into fields and groves,
bleeding into the village,
where my mother was born.

Wynn Everett

The Last Years

Maclean unmistaken,
as we two side by side,
sixty years,
flow toward oceans mouth.

My reach now depleted,
and the rippling still.
As hard though I try, no movement is stirred.

The merge began 12 months ago.

Our waters had seen the same run,
meandered the same course,
subsurface rock and obstacles,
patterned of two.

But now I do not keep pace,
his current - still down hill.
Beautiful motion, swelling and surging.
My drift weak - years of cognitive erosion,
not the vibrant river I once was,
but a silent trickle of former nights.

Yet, pulling me in,
we rush on, over rock,
sediment, crashing even mightier between banks.
Baptizing me in yesteryear
his memories – my quarry,
as he carries me home toward rivers end.

Bios

L. Ward Abel, poet, composer of music, lawyer, aspiring teacher and spoken-word performer, lives in rural Georgia, and has been published at *The Reader, The Yale Anglers' Journal, Versal, The Pedestal, Pale House, Kritya, Ditch, Open Wide, Moloch*, and hundreds of others. Abel has recently been nominated for "Best of the Web" by *Dead Mule* and *The Northville Review*. He is the author of *Peach Box and Verge* (Little Poem Press, 2003), *Jonesing For Byzantium* (UK Authors Press, 2006) and the recently released *The Heat of Blooming* (Pudding House Press, 2008).

Jennifer Ackerman is a writer of poetry and short stories from North Central Iowa where she lives with her husband and three children. She has worked as a law enforcement and 911 dispatcher for 11 years at the local sheriff's department. This is her first publication.

Tim Allen is a graduate of Rutgers University with a BA in Psychology. He is a writer of both poetry and short stories. His poetry has appeared previously in the *2007 US 1 Summer Fiction* Issue.

Glenda Barrett, a native of Hiawassee, Georgia, is an artist, poet and writer. Her paintings are on display at *Fine Art America*. Glenda's writing has appeared in *Woman's World, Chicken Soup for the Soul, Farm & Ranch Living, Rural Heritage, Psychology for Living, Nostalgia, Journal of Kentucky Studies* and many others. Her poetry chapbook titled, "When the Sap Rises," is for sale on Amazon.com, along with *"Hope Whispers,"* and *"Chicken Soup for the Soul,"* that includes one of Glenda's essays.

Mike Berger has a Ph.D. in clinical psychology and was a practicing psychotherapist for 30 years, and is now fully retired. He has authored two books of short stories, and been published in numerous professional journals, and freelanced for more than 20 years. His humor pieces *Clyde and Goliath, Good Grief Columbus*, and *If Noah Built the Ark Today* have won awards. He is now writing poetry full-time. He has many pursuits which include sculpting, painting, gardening, and baking bread.

Adam Berlin is the author of the novels <u>Belmondo Style</u> (St. Martin's Press, 2004) and <u>Headlock</u> (Algonquin Books, 2000). His stories and poetry have appeared in numerous journals. He is an Associate Professor of English at John Jay College of Criminal Justice in New York City, and co-editor of *J Journal: New Writing on Justice*.

Bob Bradshaw lives in California, where he dreams of retiring to a hammock. Recent and forthcoming work of his can be found at *Cha: An Asian Literary Journal, Writers Connect, Orange Room Review, Driftwood Review, Flutter* and *Chantarelle's Notebook*.

Bios

Regina Murray Brault's poem, "*At Either End of the Web*", was nominated for the 2009 Pushcart Prize, and was honored to receive the Angels Without Wings Foundation 2009 Vermont Senior Poet Laureate Award for her poem, "*Mother Tongue*". More than 210 of her poems have appeared in such publications as: *The Comstock Review, Midwest Poetry Review, Poet Magazine, Karamu, The State Street Review, Sacred Stones Anthology, Bloodroot Literary Magazine* and *Random House Anthology Mothers and Daughters*. Regina is the recipient of numerous poetry awards including the Clark College Poetry Award and the Tennessee Literary Award for Poetry. Her first illustrated poetry book, "*Beneath the Skin*", was released in October 2006.

Jacob M. Carpenter lives in Oregon, Illinois, a small, rural town that sits on the banks of the Rock River, about ninety miles upstream from its entrance into the Mississippi. Jacob earned his B.A. degree in creative writing from DePauw University, in Greencastle, Indiana, before attending law school at Mercer University in Macon, Georgia. After practicing law for several years, Jacob now teaches legal writing full-time at DePaul University's College of Law in Chicago. His commute is long, but he is willing to endure it so that he can live surrounded by the woods, fields, creeks, and rivers that he grew up with.

Carolyn Constable's poems have been published in *River Poets Journal* and "*The Eclectic Muse.*" anthology. Her chapbook titled, "*Carolyn's Book of Prayers,*" was published by *Lilly Press* in 2007.

Barbara Crooker's work has appeared in magazines as diverse as *Yankee, The Christian Science Monitor, Highlights for Children,* and *The Journal of American Medicine (JAMA)*. She is the recipient of the 2006 Ekphrastic Poetry Award from *Rosebud*, the 2004 WB Yeats Society of New York Award, the 2003 Thomas Merton Poetry of the Sacred Award, and three Pennsylvania Council on the Arts Creative Writing Fellowships. Her books are *Radiance*, which won the 2005 Word Press First Book competition and was a finalist for the 2006 Paterson Poetry Prize; *Line Dance*, (Word Press 2008), which won the 2009 Paterson Award for Literary Excellence; and *More* (C & R Press), which is forthcoming in 2010. She has enjoyed paddling many rivers, including the Susquehanna, the Delaware, and the Chemung.

Sally Bliumis-Dunn teaches Modern Poetry and Creative Writing at Manhattanville College. Her poems have appeared in *BigCityLit, Lumina, Nimrod, The Paris Review, Prairie Schooner, Poetry London, RATTLE, Rattapallax, Spoon River Poetry Review*. In 2002 she was a finalist for the Nimrod/Hardman Pablo Neruda Prize. Her manuscript, "Talking Underwater" was published by Wind Publications in 2007.

Bios

Wynn Everett was born in Atlanta and grew up near the Chattahoochee River. He later moved to New York where he lived along the Hudson River in Tribeca. Now he lives in Los Angeles, but comes home to visit family every year in the North Georgia Mountains on Lake Lanier. He is currently published in *Haggard and Halloo*.

Joanne Faries, originally from the Philadelphia area, now lives in Texas with her husband Ray. Published in *Doorknobs & Bodypaint, Off the Coast, Orange Room Review, and Salome magazine,* she also has stories in *Shine magazine, A Long Story Short,* and *Bartleby-Snopes*. Joanne is the film critic for the *Little Paper of San Saba*. She is a member of Trinity Writers' Workshop in Bedford, Texas.

Peter D. Goodwin lived in England until the age of eighteen; has travelled through Europe and Asia; taught at university in Thailand, and worked as a playwright. He now divides his time between New York City and the remnants of the natural world along Maryland's Chesapeake Bay. His poems have been published in several anthologies, including *September Eleven* and *Listening to the Water: The Susquehanna Water Anthology*, as well as in various journals, such as *Rattle, River Poets Journal, Delaware Poetry Review,* and *Prints*.

Cynthia Hawkins is a Ph.D. graduate of the English and Creative Writing Program at SUNY Binghamton. Her creative work has appeared in such literary journals as *Passages North, Whetstone, Stymie, and Our Stories*. Cynthia currently lives in San Antonio, Texas with her husband and two daughters and works as a freelance arts and entertainment writer.

Carole Herzog Johnston is a New Jersey Native living in the Bluegrass State. She teaches creative writing at an arts high school but spends all her spare time writing and studying haiku and other Japanese form poetry.

J. Joseph Kane is a writer, editor, and student living in Michigan. His work has previously appeared in several journals, including *Central Review, Elimae, Temenos,* and *Right Hand Pointing*. Joe grew up near a river in Michigan.

Robert S. King has been writing and publishing since the 1970s. His work has appeared in hundreds of magazines, including *The Kenyon Review, Southern Poetry Review, Lullwater Review, Chariton Review, Main Street Rag*, and others. His most recent books are *The Gravedigger's Roots* and *The Hunted River*, both from Shared Roads Press, 2009. He is currently Director of FutureCycle Press. www.futurecycle.org

Bios

Judith A. Lawrence, Editor/Publisher of *River Poets Journal/Lilly Press*. Her work has appeared in *Poet Works Anthologies, Ancient Heart, Poems for all, The River, Poetic Diversity,* and numerous online literary sites. She is currently working on a book of short stories titled *"The Art Of Living."*

Stephen Lefebure's poems have been found in corked bottles on random shores. Unrolled carefully, they may smell of old wine. Some have appeared in an anthology called *Wild Song,* and others have wandered the wilderness of small press publications for decades, appearing and disappearing periodically.

Ellaraine Lockie has received writing residencies at Centrum in Port Townsend, WA, and eleven Pushcart Prize nominations. She's been a recent recipient of the *Lois Beebe Hayna Award, the One Page Poem Prize, the Elizabeth R. Curry Prize, the Writecorner Press Poetry Award, the Skysaje Poetry Prize, the Dean Wagner Poetry Prize* and first place winner in the *Aquarium of the Pacific, California Federation of Chaparral Poets, California State Poetry Society, Green River Writers and Ina Coolbrith Circle contests.* She has also authored seven chapbooks, serves as Poetry Editor for the lifestyles magazine, *Lilipoh,* and teaches poetry/writing workshops.

Richard Mack is the author of a novel, *Quail Song* and two books of poetry and essays, *Against a Western Sky and Reflections in a Western River.* His prose and poetry have been published in numerous literary journals: *Wind Literary Review, South Dakota Review, Salal Review, Clearwater Journal, Cape Rock, Branches, Green's Magazine, Denver Post, Circus Maximus, Palouse Review, Red Lodge* and others. Mack feels at home in the American West, having lived and worked in Oregon, Colorado, Washington, California, and Idaho. His career took him to Micronesia, Guam, Japan and through-out the deserts and mountains of eastern Oregon. He lives in LaGrande, Oregon with his wife, Margo.

Thomas Michael McDade was born and raised in Pawtucket, RI. He served two hitches in the U.S. Navy, and was graduated from Fairfield University, Fairfield, CT. A resident in Monroe, CT, McDade is married without children or pets. Since 1980, he has been employed as a Business Basic Programmer in the plumbing industry. He's currently working in Meriden, CT. His poems have most recently appeared in *Main Channel Voices, Sytmie Magazine The Ester Republic, Up the Staircase. Boiling River and Zisk: The Baseball Magazine For People Who Hate Baseball Magazines.* (October 2008)

Karla Linn Merrifield, a four-time Pushcart Prize nominee and 2009 Everglades National Park Artist-in-Residence, has had poetry appear in dozens of publications as well as in many anthologies. (continued...)

Bios

She has five books to her credit, including *Godwit: Poems of Canada*, which received the 2009 Andrew Eiseman Writers Award for Poetry. She is poetry editor of *Sea Stories* and book reviewer and assistant editor for *The Centrifugal Eye* and moderator of the poetry blog, *Smothered Air*. She teaches at Writers & Books, Rochester, NY.

Dorla Moorehouse was born and raised in Ohio. She grew up with a strong awareness of the many fires that took place on the Cuyahoga River. Those stories, with their environmental warnings, shaped her identity as a native Clevelander, and have stayed with her as she moved out to Texas. "Northern Phoenix" is a meditation on the Cuyahoga fires, and their impact on Cleveland's identity.

Melissa Morris is a middle school teacher. She lives and works in New Jersey and is currently writing a middle grade novel.

Rosalie Sanara Petrouske's poetry and essays have appeared in *Southern Poetry Review, Seattle Review, Passages North, Poets On, Plainsongs, Skylark, The MacGuffin*, and other poetry journals as well as four anthologies. Her two chapbooks of poetry, The *Geisha Box and A Postcard from My Mother* were published by *March Street Press and Finishing Line Press*. She lives in Grand Ledge, Michigan, and teaches writing at Lansing Community College.

Pamela Johnson Parker is a writer, medical editor, and teacher of poetry at Murray State University. Her work has appeared in several journals. Her first chapbook, *A Walk through the Memory Palace*, won the *qarrtsiluni* chapbook contest and was published, Fall 2009.

Elijah B. Pringle, III, works in the insurance and banking industry and has held several positions mostly in training and quality. He has facilitated business and creative writing workshops and was the past editor-in-chief of IMPACT, a business periodical. To his credit are the editing and publishing of several chap books by other poets. His work will soon be published by the *Edison Poetry Review* and the *River Poets Journal*. He has already appeared on-line in "*The God's Are Bore*." He is also the former on-air host of Panoramic Poetry at October Gallery.

Anna G. Raman's work has appeared in The Guindy Times, Poetidings, The Mindful Parent website, Sangam Literary Magazine and The DuPage Valley Review. She lives in Iselin, New Jersey with her husband and daughter.

Alexandria Michelle Red Alexandria Michelle Red is a science educator, writer and a mystic from Seattle, Washington. (continued) ...

Bios

One of seven founding members of the Oratrix Spoken Word Group, she was featured on the 2003 "Oratrix" CD., and traveled as a featured artist on the 2004 All Girl. All Word. Oratrix tour. She performed nationally in theaters, festivals, cafes, bookstores, and on university campuses. She currently teaches Chemistry in Washington state. Her poetry can be found in 14 Hills, Quay, SN Review, and the Pitkin Review.

C. R. Resetarits' work has appeared in numerous journals including *Kenyon Review, Gender Studies, Fabula, Parameters, and Dalhousie Review*. "Big River" is about the river on her father's farm in Missouri. She grew up in St. Louis (mighty river). She recently moved to Washington, DC (diverse river) from the south of England (charming, chalky, easy rivers).

Dan Reynolds, Senior Editor with Risk & Insurance Magazine, based in Horsham, Pa and a former reporter for *the Pittsburgh Tribune-Review and the Pittsburgh Business Times*. His journalism has also appeared in *The Moon Record, Gambling Compliance, The Blood Horse, the Philadelphia Business Journal and the Charlotte Business Journal.* His poetry has appeared in the *Taproot Literary Review, The Loyalhanna Review, Point of Light, Wild Violet, the Pittsburgh Post Gazette,* and the *Edison Literary Review.*

Richard Roe, a retired Legislative Analyst and Editor, began writing poetry more than 30 years ago when life had stopped making sense, and has kept at it ever since. He spent his early life around the Cuyahoga (yes, Cleveland) and Ohio rivers, places he still visits several times a year. Rivers and river towns have influenced his ways of thinking all of his life. He has published three volumes of poetry with small presses and a few of his poems have appeared in periodicals.

Jenny Root of Eugene, Oregon, has had poems in *The New Southerner, Common Ground, Windfall: A Journal Poetry of Place, Poetry International, Fireweed: Poetry of Western Oregon,* and *Bellowing Ark*, and has work forthcoming in *Poets of the American West*, an anthology from *Many Voices Press*. Raised in the Detroit, Michigan area, she moved to Oregon,1989. where she worked with a number of independent booksellers and the Lane Literary Guild promoting the written word in performance. Formerly with *Story Line Press and Tsunami Books*, she now works as an editor and graphic designer with a nonprofit organization in criminal justice.

Ksenia Rychtycka's work has appeared in *Hubbub, Wisconsin Review, Alaska Quarterly Review, Driftwood: A Literary Journal of Voices From Afar,* and elsewhere. New fiction is forthcoming in *The Dalhousie Review, Yellow Medicine Review, The Literary Bohemian,* and the anthology entitled "After The Fall" by Wising Up Press. Ksenia lived in Ukraine from 1996-2000 which inspired her poem.

Bios

Tom Sheehan's books are *Epic Cures* and *Brief Cases, Short Spans*, November 2008 from Press 53; *A Collection of Friends* and *From the Quickening*, March 2009, from Pocol Press. His work is currently in many publications and in new anthologies from Press 53, *Home of the Brave, Stories in Uniform* and *Milspeak:Warriors, Veterans, Family and Friends Writing the Military Experience*.. Noted Stories for 2007 and 2008, the Georges Simenon Award for fiction, a story in the *Dzanc Best of the Web Anthology for 2009*. His novels include *Vigilantes East, Death for the Phantom Receiver* and *An Accountable Death*. His poetry books include *The Saugus Book; Ah, Devon Unbowed; and This Rare Earth & Other Flights*.

Jeanine Stevens was raised in Indiana, and currently divides her time between Sacramento and Lake Tahoe. She has four collections: "*Boundary Waters*," "*The Keeping Room*," "*The Meaning of Monoliths*," and "*Eclipse*." Her poems have been published in *Timber Creek Review, Poet Lore, Tipton Poetry Journal, and Valparaiso Poetry Review*, among others.

Ann Taylor is a Professor of English at Salem State college in Salem, Mass. where she teaches many several writing courses, including Poetry Writing, Writing about Nature, English Literature, Arthurian Literature, The Art of the Essay, and Poetry Analysis. She has written two books on college composition, academic and free-lance essays, and a collection of personal essays, *Watching Birds: Reflections on the Wing* (Ragged Mountain/McGraw Hill). Her poems have been published or accepted recently in *Arion, Ellipsis, The Dalhousie Review, Appalachia, Del Sol Review, Snowy Egret, and Classical and Modern Literture*. She lives in Woburn, Mass. with her husband, Francis Blessington.

Christopher Tiefel is a noun & verb collector & organizer. He has worked as a contributing editor for the *Wild River Review*, and now rides the R5 to Philadelphia. Words have appeared in *elimae, Strange Machines, Shoofly, and Essence*.

Mark Vogel has published articles on adolescent literacy in numerous journals for the past fifteen years. Short stories have recently appeared in /*Cities and Roads*/, /*Knight Literary Journal*/, /*Whimperbang*/ and /*Our Stories*/. Poetry appears in /*Poetry Midwest, English Journal, Cold Mountain, Cape Rock, Dark Sky,* /and other journals. He is currently Professor of English at Appalachian State University in Boone, North Carolina.

Vuong Quoc Vu was born in Saigon, Vietnam. He grew up in San Jose, CA. He studied Creative Writing at San Jose State and Fresno State Universities.

Bios

BJ Ward's most recent book of poetry is *Gravedigger's Birthday* (North Atlantic Books). His work has been featured on National Public Radio and *Poetry Daily*, as well as in publications such as *Poetry, TriQuarterly, The Sun,* and *The Pushcart Prize Anthology*. He teaches at Warren County Community College in New Jersey and lives nearby on the northern bank of the Musconetcong River.

Harry Westermeier is a soon to be retired Professional Land Surveyor for Orange County, New York. He graduated from Geneseo College with a BS in Geology. He has a love for nature and science which he tries to translate through his love of photography and poetry.

Neal Whitman, lives with his wife Elaine on the Monterey Peninsula on California's Central Coast, evenly dividing his time between writing "regular" versus haiku poems. Since 2005 he has published over 80 of each; in 2009 he won the James McIntyre Poetry Contest in Ontario, Canada and two honorable mentions in the Yuki Teikei Haiku Contest. Neal is a member of the Pacific Grove Library Advisory Board and is a volunteer tour docent at the Robinson Jeffers Tor House in nearby Carmel.

John Sibley Williams has an MA in Writing and resides in Portland, OR, where he frequently performs his poetry and studies Book Publishing at Portland State University. He is presently compiling manuscripts composed from the last two years of traveling and living abroad. Some of his over eighty previous or upcoming publications include: *The Evansville Review, Flint Hills Review, Open Letters, Cadillac Cicatrix, Juked, The Journal, Hawaii Review, Barnwood International Poetry, Concho River Review, Paradigm, Red Wheelbarrow, Aries, Other Rooms, The Alembic, Clapboard House, River Oak Review, Glass, Miranda,* and *Raving Dove*.

Christopher Woods lives in Houston and in Chappell Hill, Texas. He is a writer, teacher and photographer. His work has appeared recently in *Litchfield Review, Glasgow Review,* and in *Narrative Magazine*. He shares an online gallery with his wife Linda at *Moonbird Hill Arts* - www.moonbirdhill.exposuremanager.com/

Bill Wunder is the author of *Pointing at the Moon* (WordTech Editions, 2008) and a chapbook, *A Season of Storms* (Via Dolorosa Press, 2002). In 2004 he was named Poet Laureate of Bucks County, Pennsylvania. He was a finalist in The T. S. Eliot Prize two times, and the Allen Ginsberg Poetry Awards four times. His poems and short stories have been widely published. Bill serves as Poetry Editor of *The Schuylkill Valley Journal*, and lives with his two black labs in Bucks County.